The Joy of Writing Poetry

Create your Poemscape masterpiece

I0132527

Horace Beach Jr.

The opinions expressed in this manuscript are solely the opinions of the author and do not represent the opinions or thoughts of the publisher. The author has represented and warranted full ownership and/or legal right to publish all the materials in this book.

The Joy Of Writing Poetry
All Rights Reserved.
Copyright © <2013> Horace Beach Jr.

Images © 2012 JupiterImages Corporation. All rights reserved - used with permission.

This book may not be reproduced, transmitted, or stored in whole or in part by any means, including graphic, electronic, or mechanical without the express written consent of the publisher except in the case of brief quotations embodied in critical articles and reviews.

Dedicated

To the loving memories
of my Parents,

Pastor Veronica Beach

&

Mr. Horace Beach Sr.

The Joy of Writing Poetry

Explore the inner you

And discover the joy

Of reading and writing Poetry

Preface

My favorite three hobbies as a child growing up, were reading, writing and sketching. The act of reading and writing came naturally to me, but I was often unable to bring my sketched drawings to life with colors. I found out very early that I had a talent for scale, perspective and shadows, but my artworks were always ruined by my applications of color.

It was not until much later as an adult, that I found myself engrossed in a television show, called the **Joy of Painting,** that I was able to learn the proper techniques of applying colors to art.

I religiously tuned in or taped each weekly half hour show, in order to see the late Bob Ross, using just household paint brushes and a knife, magically transforming blank canvasses into astonishing works of art, all the while simultaneously and patiently, explaining each step of the procedure. He broke every step down into such simple terms, that myself, and others around the world, could paint along with him, as we created our own personal masterpieces. I bought all of his books, and up to this present period, I still amaze my friends with my landscape and seascape paintings. I owe it all to the **Joy of Painting** in books and videos.

That was my inspiration for creating **"The Joy of Writing Poetry"** project. Becoming aware that many people were curious about poetry, but remained noncommittal about immersing themselves into the creation of their own poetry, I have endeavored to break down the composition of poetry, into the very simplest of steps.

Acknowledgements

There are so many persons who are worthy of mention, but first and forth most are my parents and siblings. I grew up loving to read because they were always reading. My love for writing evolved from my love for reading…My inspiring family members are:

My parents: The late Pastor Veronica Beach and the late Mr. Horace Beach Sr.

My siblings: Meryl, Calvin, Winston, Beulah, Lloyd, Carol, Don and Wendy.

Special mention must be made of Wendy's husband, Bishop Malcolm Browne, who is definitely more of a brother than a brother-in-law to all of us. Also it's been always lots of fun to be goofing off with their sons, Asif, Dellon, Geron and Kadeem, all of whom have grown into responsible young adults.

The evolution of my daughter Michelle, from a baby to the magnificent adult that she is, coupled with being the wife of the outstanding Ron Whitely, and the mother of my two amazing grandchildren, Kaleese, and Ron Jr. have been, and continue to be a great source of inspiration for me.

Another worthy source of inspiration for me has been someone whom I have not met personally, but yet has been a great friend of mine for over twenty years.
We first encountered each other in the AOL chat rooms, and have been corresponding with each other ever since. Many of my poetry compositions were first sent to her for her enlightening feedbacks. Her name is Robin Roe.

Contents

The Joy of Writing Poetry
Introduction

Poetry is considered food for the soul. Ancient Greek Writers thought poetry to be the language of the Gods.

So many aspects of our everyday lives are embodied in the art form of Poetry. The human emotions of love and heartache, hope and despair, happiness and sorrow, bravery and cowardice, forgiveness and repentance, also structure and chaos, are all expressed in the language of poetry.

Poetry is indeed the heartbeat that energizes the whole rhythm of life, and if you take some time to explore it, I am certain that you would be as continually intoxicated by the art form, as I am.

Some of my own personal poems are inserted throughout the pages of this book, and are occasionally expanded on, in some detail, the steps, stages and excitement that led to their completions. However, please understand, that in the mind of a poet, a poem is never totally completed.

The increasing joy that I experience in writing and reading poetry has caused me to seek a better understanding of the fundaments of poetry. The topics that I have explored, which I now delight in sharing with you, form the basic chapters of this book.

Chapter 1:

What is Poetry?

Poetry is a whimsical explosion of emotions and dreams of observations and of enlightenments, all of which are poignantly and profoundly written.

What is Poetry?

Poetry is all around us. It is a part of every minute of every day of our lives.

It's in the songs on the radio, compact discs, or any other audio media that we listen to. When you sing or listen to a song, you are in essence, making a poetic connection. For in reality, the lyrics of the song are considered *verses* of a poem that had been set to music

The letters, emails, and newspaper articles that you wrote or read, are all in reality, a form of poetry. The juicy paperback that you just can't lay down or the E-book on your electronic tablet, the paragraphs of which are all classified as *Prose Poetry*.

PROSE POEMS are written in a paragraph and essay formats, but even if the content is fascinatingly interesting, it still seems like a bland, abstract form of poetry.

VERSE POEMS are the most recognized and popular style of poetry, the compositions of which are the basic fundaments of this book.

What is Poetry?

The architectural structure of a poem or what I call the *"PoemScape"* of a poem, is consisted of:

      (1) Title
      (2) Lines
      (3) Verses (Stanzas)

Verses/Stanzas are normally composed of two or more lines. The numbers of lines are usually consistent throughout all the stanzas comprising the poem.

Some poems, just like songs or hymns may even contain choruses. These are catchy stanzas that are replicated at equal stages throughout the poem, emphasizing the message that the poem is portraying. These chorus lines tend to be closely related to the poem's Title.

The aspects of what constitutes a poem are almost endless, but as always, it's my intention to keep this book very simple, thereby not boring you the reader with too many technical terms. However, a listing for sources of such poetry terminologies may be perused in the 'Index', at the end of this book.

Just like a short story book, a poem projects many aspects of the human condition, of our dreams and aspirations, of our growths and our downfalls, of our successes and failures, of our pasts and our futures, and of our fantasies and practicalities. However, unlike a short story, a poem condenses the journey, and so we get where we are supposed to be taken, much, much faster.

Poetry is about life, a life lived, living and to be lived. Without poetry there would be no hymns, songs, nursery rhymes, or rapping, just written short and long stories.

There would be just prose.

Poetry can elegantly and articulately document an experience that you deemed worthy to be of a poignant commemoration to be shared. Once at a family reunion, some relatives that I had not seen for some length of time and myself were sitting around a table, discussing several prevailing topics. Invariably as it sometimes do, the topic of romance came up.

Those who were in intimate relationships were asked to relate how they met and fell in love with their significant others. What unfurled, were sometimes hilarious, but most times, were very heartwarmingly uplifting and celebratory moments.

The many different ways and circumstances that love came calling, have propelled me to compose the following poem.

Love can call at any time or place

LOVE can pop suddenly out of the blue,
Or slowly creep up on you.
Please remember this is true,
That love will come when it is due.

LOVE can come calling on a bad hair day,
It can reach you when you are at work or play.
Not only when you are jolly and gay,
But also when your moods are dark and gray.

LOVE can grow slowly from a childhood friend,
Or from a stranger around the next bend.
Could it be that apprehensive blind date?
Who holds the key to your romantic fate?

LOVE blooms not only on a moonlit night,
When the stars are shining bright,
But it can come dripping out of the rain
That falls pitter patter against the window pane.

Love can call at any time or place

LOVE can find you relaxing on a tropical beach,
But rush hour in Manhattan is also within it's reach.
It may be in a single glance across the street,
Or in a Night Club rocking to a disco beat.

LOVE can come to you in the months of spring,
That is the time when the birds love to sing.
Maybe in summer with catfish jumping in the lakes,
Or during the winter amid the falling snowflakes.

LOVE can touch you at anytime or any place,
Open up your heart when it smiles in your face,
Don't question the time or the place,
Just let it wrap you in its warm embrace.

LOVE can happen anytime,
Where and when you just don't know.
It sometimes happen when you are Online,
For me personally it has been so.

What is Poetry?

Poetry has no boundaries, continually making numerous connections of persons with a host of varying backgrounds.

No boundaries

Strolling in the park one summer morn,
I saw a pretty little bird hopping on the lawn.
As I admired the honey-crowned robin,
She looked up at me and started to sing.

What happened next? I couldn't explain,
But the song she was singing echoed in my brain.
I soon found myself humming, humming her song,
We crossed over boundaries singing as one.

Amazed, I started singing a new song alone,
But she joined in at once and made it her own.
The bonding between us growing so rich and pure,
Made the difference between us unimportant for sure.

The magic of love, oh what a wondrous thing,
Leaping over boundaries with a joyous spring.
To the future we journey, with mutual respect,
Finding harmony in a world that is far from perfect.

What is Poetry?

Poetry can sometimes be an outlet to portray personal loss and grief.

The aftermath of a traumatic experience can sometimes expose a need to poetically express your deep emotional feelings, as mine did, in penning the following poem.

Guardian Angel

Guardian Angel where were you,
When my heart was being torn in two?
Were you asleep?
When you should've been awake,
To save me from this painful heartache?
Oh Guardian Angel where were you,
When my whole world
Was turning bitter, dark and blue?

We first fell in love as high school kids
And felt blessed with God in our midst.
Yet screeching tires, a teen drunk on wine,
Who in one split second,
Shattered this heart of mine.
She was so loving, so carefree and kind,
Yet her life force ended
Way before her time.

Guardian Angel

There is now a new voice
In the Angelic choir,
And the spirituals they sing
Will be an octane higher.
Yet despite my grief
I rejoice in her new Angelic birth,
For her wings were earned during
Her brief time here on earth.

Help me Guardian Angel
For I have no clue of what to do,
When I'm cloaked with pain
Like the grass with the morning dew.
My tears have dimmed the stars
In the evening sky,
Oh Guardian Angel would you please
Tell me why? Why? Why?

What is Poetry?

It's about freedom around the world

HUMANITY'S DECLARATION OF FREEDOM

TOTAL FREEDOM is not just about the right
to vocalize whatever you want to say.
Nor is it just being able to choose
where to live, to work or to play.
No, its not just a choice of being
straight or being gay.
Also its not just the right to congregate
and march in protest on any given day.
But its also about the rights of women,
for the same job as men, to receive equal pay.

    REAL FREEDOM is not just the power to vote
    for your own political candidate.
    Allowing others their own opposing view points
    do not mean that you capitulate.
    Instead, it means that the rights of self expression
    is something that you should celebrate.
    Its not just about sending your children
    to the school of your choice,
    But its also about community involvement
    and the lending of your voice.

ABSOLUTE FREEDOM is not just about the smokers
and whose personal spaces they contaminate.
Its also about the right to worship in peace,
regardless of religion or faith.
Its being mindful of the rights of invalids,
for its an isssue to which we should all relate.
Also its about ALL PEOPLE being free
to live together without all the hate.
Your freedom does not give you the right
the freedom of others to violate.......By Horace Beach (POEMSCAPES)

What is Poetry?

Poetry is all about life.

THE *abc*'s OF LIFE

A is for the ALMIGHTY, Creator of all that we know,
B is for the BIBLE, it's teachings we should follow
C is the CHARITY that we should always have for each other,
D is for the DREAMS of self-improvements that we all nurture,
E is for EDUCATION that helps to build a better future,
and F is for FAMILY, the cornerstone of our society and culture.

G is for GRANDPARENTS, they have so many stories to tell,
H is for HONESTY, HUMILITY but also HUNGER and HELL.
I is for the INVALIDS, they are INDIVIDUALS as well,
J is for JUSTICE let us all ring its bell.
K is for KINDNESS, no need to be cruel,
and L is for LOVE, it's the very first noel.

M is for MOTHER, most cherished of all,
N is for NATURE, so beautiful in the fall,
O is for OPPORTUNITIES, be ready when they call,
P is for PEACE, the pursuit of which must be perpetual,
Q is the QUEST for knowledge, both theoretical and practical,
and R is for RESPECT, not RACISM, which is irrational.

S is for SCIENCE, it's discoveries cure our ill,
T is for TIME, make haste for it never stands still,
U is for UNDERSTANDING each other, its life Cure-all pill,
V is for VICTORY, but it's the pursuit of which provides the big thrill,
W is for WISDOM of which we can never have its fill,
and X is for XMAS that we celebrate with peace and goodwill

Y is for YOU, every man, woman, boy and girl,
and Z is for the ZEAL that we should all have to improve our world.

What is Poetry?

Poetry can be funny and humorous about love.

You know, love can come wrapped up in many different packages. Many of us keep looking or waiting for a perfect partner to enter our lives. We have implanted into our minds these pre-conceived ideas of what comprises a future lifelong mate. Love, however always seem to have very flexible notions. So   please don't limit yourself by staying in that mandated mindset. We must freely entertain the idea that the people we find ourselves loving, might not fit in with those perfect visions that we have entertained. Note also, that we ourselves are not perfect. Love is not something that you find, on the contrary, love finds you. So let us all keep our minds open to love, when and where it might find us.

 The following Poem is a dramatization of love being bigger than faults themselves.

She is so easy to love

She wears high heels that make her taller than me,
And all she does each day is to spend all of my money.
Her cooking often stinks,
Her coffee no one drinks
But each day I praise the Lord above,
For she is so easy to love.

She fusses with me about the clothes that I wear,
Continually nagging about the length of my hair.
She snores when she sleeps,
And scratches me with her feet,
But holding her tight, she fits like a glove,
I find her so easy to love.

<u>She is so easy to love</u>

She dulls my blades shaving her legs,
Won't make love in the daytime however hard I beg.
Hogging the remote control with those silly talk shows,
You may wonder why she and I don't come to blows.
Fact is, she caresses my soul, gentle like a dove,
For she is so amazingly easy to love.

She steps on my toes whenever we dance,
Periodically dropping hints about a trip to France.
She won't even learn to drive our car,
And is probably the biggest klutz I know by far.
I can never look at a televised baseball game in peace at all,
For that's when she always wants a drop to the mall.
Sometimes I just want to swear Oh *#$%& Holy Cow,
But then again, she is so easy to love.

When guys flirt with her she swings her hips with a smile,
Knowing its making me jealous all of the while,
But still she gets mad all of the time
If she catches me admiring a girl who is fabulous and fine.
However, I told you then, and I will tell you now
How she is so utterly easy to love.

She is not the vision I had in my dreams,
But she found a home in my heart it seems,
And if I am coffee then she is my cream,
She is my whole life and you know what that means.
We have our ups and downs but again I vow,
That she is, oh so easy....So easy to love...

What is Poetry?

Poetry can also be defined as a written subject matter that excites all of our five senses.

(1) Sight

(2) Sound

(3) Taste

(4) Touch

(5) Smell

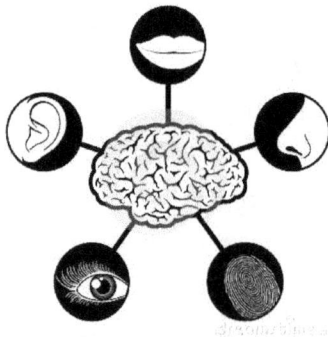

<u>Sight</u>

In our minds' eye we are able to visualize the scenery that the Poet is portraying and thus able to immerse ourselves in the unfurling story. For example, here is an insert from a poem that was part of an English Literature course, way back in my high school days

The Poem's title is "**<u>The Highway Man</u>** ",
by Alfred Noyes (1880-1958)

Quote:"*The road was a ribbon of moonlight
over the purple moor,
And the highway man came riding, riding*".

End of quote.
Now, physically I have never been to Scotland, but in that instant, I was mentally transported there. I imagined a narrow, winding road made visible by the moonlight, even amidst the purple covered moor.

In describing a sunset scene, the following lines may also cause the poem to tap into your inner sight.

"*The entire western hemisphere appeared to be illuminated
By a vast variety of colorful Christmas bulbs*"

Yes, poetry taps into our inner sight.

<u>Sound</u>

"We first fell in love as high school kids
And felt blessed with God in our midst.
Yet screeching tires, a teen drunk on wine,
Who in one split second,
Shattered this heart of mine".

Above is an insert from one of my poems,
"Guardian Angel" It was my desire to have the readers look
sharply around at the horrifying sound of screeching tires, to
be all involuntary witnesses in the scene, as a result of an
indication of sound.

Taste

Videos or pictures of delectable edibles can sometimes cause your mouth to water involuntarily, similarly, so can a poet tease your taste buds. A poet once caused me an imaginary taste of sprayed sea salt, as the poet wrote about the waves smashing repeatedly against the rocks, below where the poem's characters were standing, which then caused sea foam to splash into their faces.

Certain lines in poems can induce a bitter taste on your lips. Such is the remarkable effect that poems have, to be able to mentally excite your sense of taste in a very magical way.

<u>Touch</u>

Stanzas that may have been built around the following lines, can indeed conjure up unreal sensations of touching and being touched.

"The cobbled stones beneath my feet"

"The gentle caress of the early morning breeze"

"My heart fluttered by the soft touch of her lips against mine"

"So impressed was I by the firm handshake"

"The old blanket felt gritty and itchy against my skin".

A poem indeed has the power to bring the seemingly real sensations of touch, not only to your body, but they may also be heartfelt.

Smell

Once again, an insert from Alfred Noyes's poem,
"The Highwayman" tickles your senses, this time, one of smell.

Quote:
"He rose upright in the stirrups; he scarce could reach her hand,
But she loosened her hair, the casement! His face burnt like a brand
As the black cascade of perfume came tumbling over his breast;
And he kissed its waves in the moonlight".
 End of quote:

The above inserts provide a powerful sense of smell by the "Black
cascade of perfume", of her loosened hair.

In many poems, a poet can command a sense, such as there is a smell of
the coming spring in the air, or cause your nostrils to flare in response
to the written tantalizing scent of a bouquet of flowers.

The poet may even cause your nose to twitch, at the scribing mention of
raw sewage and garbage in the alleyways of some ancient settlement.

Sometimes also, the smell of fear or the sweet smell of success can be
conjured up into our minds, by the written words in a poem.

What is Poetry?

Poetry is Spiritual.

Poetry is Therapeutic.

Poetry is Educational.

Poetry is Emotional

Poetry is a Celebration.

Poetry is about Romance

Poetry is Spiritual

The spiritual goodness derived from poetry cannot be denied.
How less enjoyable would our Church and Sunday school services
be, without the inspiring songs and old hymnals? The old Gospel
songs that we learnt as kids, still cling with little effort, to our
memories, practically word for word and melody for melody.

These lines of old poetry have admittedly been the base of
inspiration for our modern poets, songwriters and rappers.

Poetry is Therapeutic

The many benefits of poetry are limitless in scope. The Internet and its many search engines, freely allow us to search for any type of poetry that appeals to our changing moods. At the clicking of a computer mouse, and the tapping on a smart phone or an electronic pad device, can almost instantly display a list of poetry, from which a particular one can be read. Ones that can possibly inspire, heal, enhance awareness, and lift or soothe whatever our prevailing psyche may be, at any time or place.

Poetry is Educational

Old Nursery Rhymes are given new lives by our kids and their electronic learning devices. The new age of animation has not only revitalized the old nursery rhymes, but also has given birth to a host of new ones, which as we all know, play a great part in the development and learning process of the young minds.

In all levels of institutional education, our English Literature classes introduced us to the works of the best poets in history.

The publications of William Shakespeare, Emily Dickinson and Oscar Wilde, just to mention a few, have given us a great insight into human history, human culture and human creativity. Our lives have been and will forever be enriched by their excellent contributions to our English literature.
Many of our imminent authors and play writers have cited these past and present literary giants, as their inspirations, and who now continue the process of inspiring others, including myself.

Poetry is Emotional

Poetry has the uncanny knack of making us laugh or cry, occasionally both at the same time. It can sometimes make us want to go out and be by ourselves to either sulk or contemplate our world and our place and function in it. Other times, it might make us either want to bond with old friends, or to go out and make new ones.

Poetry is a Celebration

This specialty aspect of poetry helps us to celebrate the meaningful periods of our civilization. We joyfully experience the different phases of our existence with a variety of literature that depict the seasons of Spring, Summer, Fall and Winter, as well as the special days of births, growths, graduations, weddings, anniversaries, valentine and a host of other Spiritual days of wonder.

It's constantly amazing to me how tightly woven into every aspect of our society, is the art form of poetry.

Poetry is about Romance

The aspect of romance is probably the most favorite and most widely understood characteristic of poetry. There is scarcely a need to further qualify the preceding statement, unless it is with the following poem.

THE abc's OF LOVE

A is for the ABUNDANCE of love that we share,
B is the BALCONY from which I would serenade you, my Dear
C is for the COMMITMENT between us that is so very sincere,
D is the DELIGHT I feel whenever you are near,
E is the EXCITEMENT that you bring to my life with such a great flair,
and F is for our FUTURE together that promises to be bright and clear.

G is for the GENTLE nature that God gave to you,
H is for my HEART filled with a love so true,
I is for our INTIMACY that is always so fresh and new,
J is for the JUKEBOX that still plays the songs we love dancing to,
K is the KINDRED spirit that bonds us like glue,
and L is the LIGHT your love shines on me when I am feeling blue.

M is for the MEMORIES shared, that we can always replay,
N is for the NURTURING of our love so that it grows more each day,
O is our OPTIMISM eternal, that our lives won't go astray,
P is for my PLEDGE of honor comes whatever may,
Q is for the QUIET time we take to honor God and pray,
and R is the RESPECT that provides a solid foundation, and its not a cliche.

S is for SWEETHEART, the endearment that springs to my lips with a sigh,
T is the TEARS of joy that fill my eyes whenever you see me cry,
U is the UNDERSTANDING between us, its the binding tie,
V is for VALENTINE, you will be mine until I die,
W is the WRONG WORD you'll never hear me say, and that is good-bye,
and X is the XEROX of you, I hope our kids will be when the time comes nigh.

Y is for YOU, my dream that came true,
and Z is for the ZILLION kisses that I will be wanting from you.

Copyright © 2001 Horace Bush

Chapter 2:

How to write poetry

If you can compose a letter,
Then you can write a poem.

An artist collects a wide variety of color paints in order to create a masterpiece. Words, life experiences and an imagination are the only ingredients needed to compose a poem, as a poet paints a picture with words.

How to write Poetry: Introduction

In order to write poetry, one must read a lot. The books read, must be on a wide variety of subjects and by a wide variety of authors. The prospective poets must be very conversant with as many aspects of the past and present world that we inhabit. To that effect, the budding writer must also read as many magazines and newspaper articles as possible.

I most definitely suggest that you acquaint yourself with books written by Zane Grey. His books about romance in his stories of the Old West are filled with very vivid descriptions of western landscapes, skylines and amazing sunsets.

Always try to make it a habit to have a handy writing pad, whenever you are reading anything at all, be it a book, magazine or a newspaper. Jog down words that you do not understand, with the intention of finding their meanings later. It's also very important to write down words that you find fascinating, words that peak your interest. Please note that to authors and poets, the storyline or subject matter can be categorized as being their cannon, but words are definitely considered their ammunition. Whereas authors have many paragraphs and pages to unravel their tales, poets have only a limited number of measured verses to process and embody their topical matter.

I cannot stress enough the importance of building up your own written and easily available repertoire of **special words**.

The best way to learn how to write poetry is to read a lot of poetry, from as many different poets as you can. Their works can offer great insights into topical subjects, verse building, rhyming and styles.

In keeping with my theme of keeping this book very simple in nature, I will be proposing some uncomplicated **poetry writing exercises** at various points throughout the remainder of this book.

How to write Poetry

Rhyming

All great poems do not necessarily have to rhyme, but my personal preference, is to compose those that do. Therefore rhyming will play a large part in the upcoming exercises.

Remember, all of your favorite songs and melodies are simply poems that had musical notes written for them. Their rhythmic rhyming enhances the appeal of the melodies, and renders the lyrics much more easily remembered.

Poetry writing Exercises

Exercise 1: Rhyming: This is achieved when adjacent lines or semi-adjacent lines of a poem ends with a similar sounding syllable. Some poets rhyme up to four or more adjacent lines, but if this is not done properly, the poem gets to be a little monotonous. Other poets may choose to just rhyme the last two lines in a verse, as a means of adding some sort of exclamation or climax to each verse. However, Rhyming two adjacent lines or every other one is most common.

In an extract from one of my poems below, I knew that I wanted that first line to end with "*flavor*", so I jogged down words, with those starting in alphabetical order, (A), (B), (C), etc, etc. That is words that rhyme with "*flavor*".

Words like Anger, Behavior, Caper, Donor, Gator,
Until I got to Nature.
Rhyming Name with "Same" was very easy.

The sound of her voice was a tantalizing flavor,
Musically Caribbean, in its endearing nature.
Now being called by another will never be the same,
As that moment when she first called my name.

Do not use a rhyme word simply because it rhymes, it also has to make sense in the overall theme. Earlier I wrote about building up a reservoir of special words, ones that you find particularly fascinating. I further encourage you to find and record several words that rhyme with those intriguing **special** words. You can create a personal dictionary of your own special words with their rhyming counterparts. These words always come in handy, especially when you are suffering word lock, while composing a poem.

How to write Poetry

A subject matter that is written in prose, that is, in an essay format can be considered a form of poetry. Converting that content into lines of lyrics is a very important exercise in learning to compose poems.

Exercise 2: Extracting from Prose:

Extract a section that you find particularly interesting in a book, magazine or a newspaper article, and try to contract it in your own words, to a series of line sentences of four to six lines, without losing the original essence of it. Try to maintain a uniform length of syllables in each line. The next step would be to establish a rhyming sequence.

You must make an effort to work on this exercise as often as you can. Try recalling an old email that you sent or received, in which the subject matter was an apt description of a place visited, or an occurred incident, as such would be totally suitable for this type of exercise.

How to write Poetry

In the previous exercise it revealed that much can be learnt about poetry composition by converting prose into lines of poetry. Likewise, much can also be gained by going in the reverse direction, that is, by turning lyrical lines into prose.

I refer to this as, Reverse Poetry Engineering.

Exercise 3: Reverse Poetry Engineering:

This particular exercise can prove to be lots of fun for anyone who loves to write. This time, take any poem that appeals to you, and write a small **prose paragraph** or two on the essence that you personally derived from it. A good study of both efforts would definitely increase your skill at composing poems.

How to write Poetry

Songs often tell a story about a subject that touches you on some emotional level, and at the end of the song you can sometimes be left wanting more lyrical content.
The next exercise seeks to address this sometime prevailing issue.

Exercise 4: Non-official Lyrical Add Ons:

How often have you been so moved and captivated by the lyrics of a song, that when the song was concluded, you were always left lamenting that it ended too soon, and wishing that there were more additional verses. I regularly find myself in this predicament when I am listening to Country and Western music, which happens to be my favorite musical genre.

Your task in this exercise is to try composing at least one extra verse to any of your favorite songs, of course keeping within the songwriter's general scheme. Be sure to maintain the number of syllables in your lyrical lines as those of the original. I can see you having lots of fun with this project. You can even privately refer to the results of your efforts as the **"missing verses"**.

How to write Poetry

Real life issues are definitely fertile grounds for the germination of poetic expressions.

Exercise 5: **Real life Connections:** I would suggest writing at least a paragraph or two about a personal incident, either happy or sad, that occurred in your life. You would then try transforming such paragraphs, first into single line sentences, and then further refine them into lines of rhyme. My parents were married for over fifty years, and when my mother died, my eight other siblings and myself, reunited from different parts of the world to grieve her passing, which occurred on Valentine Day. It was a year to that day that I sat down and wrote a memorial Valentine Poem to Mom.

.

Valentine Poem to Mom

To Mom (our vote for Mother of the Century)

Dear Valentine, please let your arrow fly
With its eternal message of love
To our dear Mother, at her home in the sky
One year has gone by
Though we still hurt and sometimes we cry
We can't bring ourselves to say goodbye.
Mom, you are alive in our hearts each and everyday
A sweet vision in our dreams and also when we pray
When temptation comes calling urging us to do wrong
We sense your presence helping us to resist and be strong
So even though, the tears come and go
Whenever we think of you we will simply say hello
Ours are not to reason why
But please don't ask us to say goodbye
We now join hands across the ocean
To give you one more standing ovation
Following your path of faith and inspiration
Is our mutual life long resolution
We hope this message reaches across space and time
To let you know that you will always be our Valentine

Horace A. Beach Jr.
New York, NY

How to write Poetry

The importance of creating a captivating title cannot be overstressed.

<u>Exercise 6:</u> Create a catchy Title: All of us are often drawn to sample or and investigate movies, songs and books by their interesting or topical titles. Numerous great subject matters are sometimes overlooked because of a less than captivating title. Similarly, poetry requires a magnetic factor in attracting attention from the general masses.

The title must grab the readers' attention just like the name of an amusement park draws in spectators to its spectacular rides. Consider that you want to write a poem about something that occurred on one of your walks to your home. The title "THE WALK HOME" may instantly spring to your mind. However, in regards to your theme, the following titles may be more attention grabbing.

> (1) The Thrilling Walk Home
> (2) It Was A Walk Home To Remember
> (3) The Chilling Walk Home

I am pretty sure that you may already have some subject matter that you want to write about, so your exercise is to compose some fascinating titles for them.

In the upcoming poem, I wanted to write about cheating at love and its usual sad consequences, but also of regret and self reclamation. After thinking long and hard about a title, the "THE DARK SIDE OF THE HEART" tumbled into my mind. I then composed a poem based on the catchy title.

Sometimes the poem is derived from the title, other times the title gives birth to the poem. This is what is so exciting and joyful about writing poetry, you can never always anticipate the writing process.

The Dark Side of the heart

The dark side of the heart is a terrible place to dwell.
It's like living in the city of pain the capital of hell.
Every awful breath that you try to take,
Is like being tormented with a sharp wooden stake.
It's a place haunted by unanswered dreams,
In which each of your broken promises rants and screams.
Ghostly echoes of the many lies you told,
Parade relentlessly across your naked soul.

Bombarded mercilessly by your weak alibis
That ripped apart the fabric of your lover's ties.
The bright light of joy from your life departs,
When you are exiled on THE DARK SIDE OF THE HEART.
You see I once floated serenely on the illuminated side,
And was given all the love that a happy heart can abide.
I basked joyfully in the completeness of her love,
It was like being wrapped comfortably in a velvet glove.

Constantly cheating I took for granted the love that she gave,
Being repeatedly selfish her sweet love I could not save.
Sadly I now realize that falling in love is just the start,
But staying in love involves the mind and the heart.
My selfish love did not last very long,
But an honest commitment would've kept the unity strong.
I deserve to be here totally marooned from the light,
But I aim to redeem myself with deeds that'll shine bright.

Turning my life around I will make an exemplary art,
So I can be released from the DARK SIDE OF THE HEART.

How to write Poetry

The opening line to a poem rivals the title in overall importance in capturing the attention of the reader.

Exercise 7: The opening line:

The opening line to your poem should be as dramatic, as a prelude to a show. It should make the reader wonder what comes next. Whereas the title must grab the readers' attention, the opening line's task is to guide them into the realm of your poem. The openingline can be rendered with a statement or a question.

You should research some great historical opening lines and then try reinventing them with your own flavor. Do you recall the one written by Charles Dickens?

"It was the best of times it was the worst of times"

Imagine that line being transformed into
"Hope for the future despite stormy echoes of the past".

It would be a good exercise to grasp and record some existing opening lines, then from them, try to create new opening lines, but with an opposite sentiment.

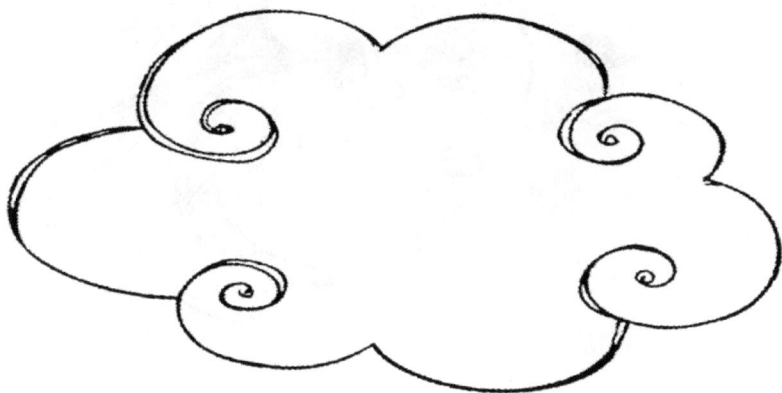

How to write Poetry

Success in any assignment undertaken is greatly enhanced by prior research on the subject matter.

<u>Exercise 8:</u> Research: The internet as we know, is an unlimited source of information on a wide variety of subject matter. The use of GOOGLE or any other search engines can lead to similarly expressed emotions, incidents or experiences, in prose or poetry formats.

This specialized research can help you to further analyze, organize and streamline your thoughts and ideas in a more cohesive manner.

How to write Poetry

Constant revision, that is, the re-evaluating of composed lines is very important.

<u>Exercise 9:</u> Revision: As you would have now realized, that not many poems are written in one sitting. You should therefore make it a practice to occasionally peruse all your earlier efforts, as some new awareness about a previous attempt, may dawn on you.

These new insights may be about additional lines or the re-phrasing of existing ones. They may even be about a total revision, of taking the budding poem into a new direction.

Constantly re-reading the lines, first silently, then aloud, can indeed open up new avenues of thought.

How to write Poetry

The sharing of your early efforts with someone who can give an unbiased opinion, is also very important in the writing process.

Exercise 10: **Sharing and Posting:** At some stage in the development of your poems, you would need to share them with someone close to you. It should be a person or persons of whom you are certain can provide you with critical appraisements of your efforts.

Now while these appraisements must be seriously evaluated by you, don't ever let your desire to continue to write, be swayed by these comments, whether they are of a positive or negative nature. Remember, any kind of feedback is good, and is something that can be taken to heart and to build on.

Later on, you should open up your efforts to a wider group of people, in an effort to solicit a greater variety of comments.

Also take some tentative steps of posting some of you efforts on facebook or any other of your other favorite social networks. Feedbacks of any kind can only help to develop your composition skills.

Chapter 3:

When and Where To Write Poetry?

Anytime or any place.

When or Where to Write Poetry

There is no special time or place to write poetry. In fact, poems often choose their own times of conceptions. A poem is seldom completed in one sitting.

Poetry springs from our imaginations, and that is something that we all endowed with. Imagination coupled with a desire to write, and together powered by constant blasts of inspiration can certainly give birth to creative poetry.

Inspirational subjects for poems unfurl around us continuously and are totally varied in their compositions. They can parade in the humorous antics of a child or a pet, or from observing acts of courage or kindness on your way to work or school. A beautiful landscape, a starry or stormy night, an article in the news about an incident happening half way around the world, can be sources of inspirations for the aspiring poet. I have occasionally drawn inspiration from other peoples' poems and songs, by being driven to articulate an opposing or parallel view to that posed by the writer.

Unlike an artist who occasionally has to tote a variety of equipment to his or her place of inspiration in order to paint the desired scene, a poet requires only a pencil and a notebook when a subject matter presents itself. The writer can jot down the main points of the arresting thought, which could be fleshed out right there and then, or at a later time.

Even if it's just a potential title for new poem that is brought to my awareness, I would write it down along with a note about what triggered it. Sometimes this occurs on my subway commute to work then on my lunch break. Later on I would try to build on it.

When or Where to Write Poetry

Weddings, funerals, christenings, and other social gatherings are often unexpected sources of inspirations for the poet. I have also known writers, who having just returned from vacation, immediately begun frantic sessions of poetry compositions, completely energized by the numerous stimuli of their holiday adventures.

Several years ago, I visited my brothers and sisters in West Palm Beach, Miami. They are all Christians in the Pentecostal faith. My brother-in-law happens to be the Bishop and leader of their church. A visitor came by, and my sister, also a Pastor, introduced her to me. She happened to be a young lady from the Caribbean island of Jamaica, and her name is Blossom. While I was thinking what a beautiful and poetic name it was, I noticed that she appeared to be genuinely shy.

It was later at a church service that I saw her again. She was called upon to lead a program, and with a mike in her hand, I was astonished to see how she blossomed into a confident articulate person, and completely at ease with her spirituality.

So overtaken was I by her blossoming before my very eyes, that I was driven to compose a poem, about the heart of a blossom.

I now share this poem with you.

The Heart of a Blossom

There is a place that I discovered not too long ago,
Where anyone can see an amazing beauty show.
No more wondrous sight you will ever see,
As in the heart of a blossom and its emerging beauty.

There are so many natural beautiful wonders to be seen,
Like a moonlit night and its starry gleam.
But to be in the heart of a blossom as its beauty unfolds,
Is like no other sight that you can imagine or behold.

Transplanted from Jamaica and here under the sun and moon,
Is a delicate Blossom that is just about ready to bloom.
Possessing a quality so gentle, so rare, so divine,
Her emerging beauty will certainly stand the test of time.

Invited into the blossoming portals of her heart,
The world's greatest picture show is about to start.
Her petals will unfold as if ready to fly,
I'm hoping to be embraced by her beauty until I die.

When or Where to Write Poetry

Everyone has their own favorite period of the day or the week, which is normally referred to as their time. There is also special place that they go to be by themselves to relax, or to meditate, or to contemplate their lives and their general place in the total scheme of things. Such times and places can prove to be fertile grounds for the germination and propagation of poems.

During the infrequent lull of babysitting, or even while looking at shows on television, the idea of a poem can manifest itself into your consciousness. Always be ready with your notebook to jot it down.

There is also a quiet period between the end of your last favorite television show at night, and the time that you fall asleep. That is the time when you think about how the day had gone, and of your plans for the next coming day. It's also a great time for the formation or continuation of a poem.

Remembering once again it is very seldom that a poem is completed in one sitting. Personally, I normally have thirty or more poems in different stages of construction.

When or Where to Write Poetry

Regrettably, there are times when some major tragedy occurs somewhere around the world, and on that awful day, September 11th 2001, it happened in New York City. Many, including myself, found it therapeutic to compose poems about that dreadful event.

Here is one of mine.

A bad New York Day
: God bless America:

The morning was the beginning of a bright and sunny day,
One full of promise for those at work or at play.
Suddenly out of the blue,
The winged bird of metal flew.
Not into the wide open skies,
Where it normally flies.
Instead it dove straight into the landmark cage,
Where many a worker earned a wage.
It struck from out of the clear blue sky,
And so many people had to die.
So surreal, like in a movie it seemed,
But this was real life, it was not a dream.

We stood stunned at this apparent accident,
But before our instant horror was totally spent,
We witnessed the escalating tragedy unfurling,
For another plane was headed straight for the tower's twin.
Crashing into the structure with a sonic boom,
That spelled for many, an instant doom.
Yes, dealing death, therein and down below,
Pedestrians scrambling to escape the shrapnel flow.
It then rapidly dawned on our minds sublime,
That this incident was not accident of any kind.
But was in fact, a terrorist act,
At this cowardly attack we will certainly react.

We watched, we waited, the long day has just begun,
Another hijacked plane had struck the Pentagon.
Hundreds of innocent passengers forced to become torpedo bombs.
Now lost in the debris are brothers, sisters, dads and moms.
Emergency teams are among the countless casualties,
And survivors stumble blindly with echoes of help me please.
Amid the flames, the smoke, the victims and the grime,
New York and America stood united against this awful crime.
A blow against America and freedom had just been cast,
Our response will be harsh and it will be fast.
Terrorists all over must be eradicated once and for all,
Even if their evil, supporting governments are made to fall.

Television media displayed many riveting scenes,
Painful as they were, we could not turn away by any means.
The awful vision of people flying thru empty air,
Will be forever be imprinted in our memories each and every year.
My coworkers screamed and as I turned around,
Saw a tower rapidly tumbling to the ground.
I could not help the tears from streaming down my face,
Knowing that we'd just witnessed needless death taking place.
What I just cannot seem to understand,
Is man's sometimes inhumanity to his fellow man.
But today the world over united as one and as such was the case,
Then there is a bright beacon of hope for the human race.

When or Where to Write Poetry

Regularly after a tragedy occurs, we observe the emergence of heroes out of ordinary people. On that awful day in New York, many arose from the city's three emergencies services. Such were their sacrifices, determinations and courage that I was inspired to write a poem dedicated to their unbelievable efforts.

Heroes at large (NYPD-NYFD-NYEMS)

You lived your lives always on a razor's edge,
Simply because you made a lifelong pledge,
To aid, protect and serve us all,
And when disaster came you promptly answered the call.

Duty bound to fight FIRE, ILLNESS and CRIME,
Your heroics flood our hearts and our minds.
Here in the greatest city of the world,
None are ever as brave or as bold.

In an undeclared war you number among the casualties,
Unimaginable grief suffered by your families.
So many brave partners buried in the grime,
But their lights of sacrifice will shine for all time.

In the midst of our sorrow you gave us hope,
Working in ground zero, eyeballing the awful scope,
Placing your personal grief and loss on hold,
Toiling endlessly in the day's heat and the night's cold.

Batman and Spiderman should be seeking your autographs,
For the men of New York's finest, walk a true hero's path.
Let us all clap hands and sing songs on your behalf,
Hip-Hip-Hurray for the City's three finest staffs.

When or Where to Write Poetry

The Christmas season always brings a bunch of happy tidings to families and friends. It's a time for Santa Claus and gifts to be given and received. Internet purchasing makes this a much easier task, so I thought about updating the adventures of Santa Clause, in a poetic tale about how Santa has gone cyber.

SANTA HAS GONE CYBER

SANTA HAS GONE CYBER, he is so daring and bold,
He has brought his reindeers in from the cold,
Now children everywhere are certain to login,
To be checking the contents of their digital stockings.
Yea, he is buzzing computers in every household,
Yet these, his Internet visitations had never been foretold.
His magic is beyond what anyone knows,
Being instantaneously everywhere the Internet flows.
From AOL, AMAZON, YAHOO or INTERNET EXPLORER
Santa's Sleigh lights seem to bathe you in their glow.
*Yes, regardless of which **dot.com** you may go,*
You are bound to hear his merry laughter of Ho, Ho, Ho.

His bag is chock full of goodies, beyond compare,
You can email your orders from sites everywhere.
Just by tapping your keyboard and clicking your mouse,
It will influence Xmas celebrations throughout your house.
SANTA HAS GONE CYBER, he is so dashing and bold,
He is making a giant leap into the future from days of old.
I am emailing Santa, requesting that he sends,
Many Christmas greetings to all of my friends.
I cannot be with you all at this time of year.
So may his download bless you all with lots of Christmas cheers?

SANTA HAS GONE CYBER, he is shopping around,
He is influencing prices that keep tumbling down.
Don't just check your chimneys hoping for a sight,
Thru Microsoft windows, you might glimpse him that night.
For SANTA HAS GONE CYBER, he is surfing full tilt,
So on Christmas Eve, I'll scan in a picture of cookies and milk.
SANTA HAS GONE CYBER, you'd better believe it's true,
He will bring your loved ones, closer to you
SANTA HAS GONE CYBER, he is way beyond bold,
So now his NEW legendary journeys can finally be told.....

When or Where to Write Poetry

During our pensive moments when we are alone, we often find ourselves reflecting on our relationships with our friends, including those that may be of a social or intimate nature. It's virtually impossible not to analyze and to form certain conclusions.

Relationships are constantly evolving, so often times these pensive moments inspire me to write about life, love and friendships.

Here is one I wrote about the connection between friends and sweethearts.

Friends and Sweethearts

Learn to be friends with your Sweetheart,
That is if you want your Love to last.
Take a good look at friendship
And tell me what you know,
Friends will last a lifetime,
While lovers come and go.

Love is not always sweet and perfect,
It can flash hot and it can idle cold.
Friendship is the warmth between that can protect,
And keep it shining solid as gold.
So if you want your love to last,
Learn to be friends with your Sweetheart.

Love is like being on a roller coaster ride,
With ups and downs and bumps and swerves.
The virtues of friendship will coincide,
To level the hills and straighten the curves.
So if you want your love to last,
Learn to be friends with your Sweetheart.

Being in love is sweet and that is no mistake,
But when friendship is involved for goodness sake,
Well, that's like having the proverbial icing on the cake,
Which will empower your love life to go from good to great.

You see, friendship is the glue,
That will forever bind your love closer to you.
So if you don't want you and your love to part,
Then you must learn to be friends with your Sweetheart.

When or Where to Write Poetry

The pensive moments of my life always seem to trigger an urge to write about love. Here is another about infinite love.

*BEYOND
FOREVER MORE*

BEYOND FOREVER MORE

Will I always love you?
Honey, I am not quite sure.
I will love you forever and ever
But who can tell what's beyond forevermore.

I will always be at your side,
From now until eternity,
But past that time hangs a curtain,
Beyond which I just cannot see.

Just let us live and love each other,
And be as happy as we can be,
So that when we get to the door beyond forever,
To open it, our love just might be the key.

May our days be many
In this world that we know,
And from within our hearts
May these joyous feeling ever flow.

We can build a bridge to the future,
For others in love to follow,
So that romance will continue to glow,
Into the most furthest of tomorrow.

I love you now,
I will love you forevermore,
But what's beyond that time,
Only God knows for sure.

When or Where to Write Poetry

When our armed forces are call upon to protect freedom, human life and dignity, usually halfway around the world, there are certain personal issues that we all have to confront. The most forthright of which is the danger that our loved ones face in their deployments to these hotspots. Most headlines are about the male member who is at risk, the son, husband, father, brother or the boyfriend.

However, times have changed, and an increasing number of females are now being deployed overseas. Consequently, they are occasionally added to the list of casualties.

Lots of poetry has been written during and about times of war.

My next super long poem covers the anguish of a husband, whose wife is a naval officer on a warship that had been deployed to the Gulf, during Operation Desert Storm.

Stormy Rose

I burst thru the front door calling out her name,
Closing the door on the thunder, lightning, and the rain.
Happy anniversary darling, I bet you can't even guess
What I bought for you when I was over in Budapest.
Reaching into my pocket I was suddenly filled with dread,
For all that I extracted, was just the receipt instead.
My mind now bordering between sane and insane,
Realizing I must have left her gift back on the plane.

Ignoring her pleas I went back out into the rain and the wind,
It's our first anniversary she deserves a very special something.
Staggering to a flower shop just about to close its doors,
Went in and bought her the last single red rose.
Rushing back home as fast as the storm would let me,
Keeping the double wrapped rose as safe as safe can be.
Leaping into my arms crying that she was frightened so much,
And just knowing how much I loved her was gift and gift enough.

This she said will always be my STORMY ROSE,
I will treasure it, until my life comes to a close.
Remembering forever how it came in out of the storm
Calming me with all of your love in it's most perfect form.
So no matter how hard the gale wind of life blows,
My trust is in your love and my red STORMY ROSE.

Being a female Naval Officer, it soon came to dawn,
She was called upon to protect freedom in Operation Desert Storm.
Before embarking, she placed a package into my hand,
Take care of it she said, I'll be back as soon as I can.
Inside the package, vacuum sealed, was her rose,
Perfect and protected as if it had just been froze.
I tried to be brave though I knew I was fooling no one,
Just wanting to keep her safe in my arms where she belongs.
Don't worry she says, this is the life that I chose,
So place your faith in God and this, my STORMY ROSE.

This she said will always be my STORMY ROSE,
I will treasure it, until my life comes to a close.
Remembering forever how it came in out of the storm
Calming me with all of your love in it's most perfect form.
So no matter how fierce the wind of war blows,
My safety lies in your love and my red STORMY ROSE.

She was among the first of the war casualties
Her plane shot to pieces over the stormy seas.
Hope for survival was very slim at best.
As search and rescue teams were bravely put to the test.
Dear Lord I prayed, don't let this be,
Please find my love and bring her safely back to me.
Looking over her package, I kept my eyes closed,
So that my tears of despair would not fall on the rose.
Refocusing on it, I then remembered what she said,
And hope sprung eternal where it once had been dead.
The word soon came around that she had been found,
Clinging with others to wreckage, shocked, but safe and sound.
Thank you, I said to her red STORMY ROSE,
How it somehow affected her safety, God only knows.

This she said will always be my STORMY ROSE,
I will treasure it, until my life comes to a close.
Remembering forever how it came in out of the storm
Calming me with all of your love in it's most perfect form.
Lost at sea amid the huge swells and endless flows,
My faith was in your love and my red STORMY ROSE.

When or Where to Write Poetry

Several years ago while listening to a lecture on the foundation of music, significant mentions were made about musical chords. The "C" chord in particular.

My literary buttons suddenly began pulsating as I recalled the idea that was floating around in my mind, about the foundation of love, centered around words that begun with the letter "C". These words are as follows

        (1) Connection
        (2) Commitment
        (3) Communication
        (4) Compromise
        (5) Collaboration
        (6) Compassion

Suddenly it clicked, why don't I combine the foundation of music with the foundation of love? Thus a poem about the C-notes of love came into being.

.

C-NOTES OF LOVE

Love is the music of life,
its the melody in a song,
Striking the C-NOTES of love
would really help it along.

CONNECTION: Connecting with one's own soulmate is our greatest desire,
blending in unison like the voices of a choir.
For when two people make a connection, falling in love as one,
they cast a light that shines way out into eternity and beyond.

COMMITMENT: Falling in love is easy, but it is just the very start,
but committing to loving, involves the mind and the heart.
A selfish love may bring you pleasure but it wont last very long,
a commitment to each other's desires keeps the unity strong.

COMMUNICATION: Too many former happy homes often go on sale,
due to lack of communications or some sorry tall tales.
We must communicate our true thoughts and feelings at all times,
and never going to sleep with anger lingering on our minds.

COMPROMISE: In all loving relationships compromising must be done,
so that just not the same partner's activities receive all the action.
You may give up something but you'll get something back in return,
for in love, the giving and receiving is of mutual and beneficial concern.

COLLABORATION: Joint ventures must always be planned as a group,
for collaboration will keep you from ending up in hot soup.
Each others views must be taken into account,
so that joy would be mutual in major amounts.

COMPASSION: No one is perfect, this we all know to be true,
So compassion is needed when ideas or plans fall through.
Try and try again must be your rallying cry,
a show of support and consideration will help them get by.

Striking the C-NOTES of love are easy to hit,
we must endeavor to learn them all, bit by bit.
For only thru them will lovers get along,
filling their lives with rapture like the melody in a song.

Copyright © 2001 Horace Beach

When or Where to Write Poetry

During the early hey days of the internet chat rooms, and now on all the social networks, like facebook and twitter, are now venues where we all have struck up numerous online acquaintances. The variety of topics discussed, as well as shared experiences, can often inspire a host of topics for the formation of poems. The following poem is dedicated to a very special internet friend of mine.

FACELESS

FACELESS

Are you an Angel sent from the heavens above,
To teach this lonely man all about love?
The melody of your song lingers in the air,
With a message of hope, so abundantly clear.

Your face unseen, does not matter to me,
My heart knows what is more important to see,
And that is kindness, respect and sweet sincerity,
Mixed with fun and laughter, it's your reality.

You are in my dreams each and every night,
Also during the day, when the sun is shining bright.
My heart is always poised to take flight,
And soar with you to love's majestic heights.

So who are you, woman without a face,
Whom every second my thoughts embrace,
Whose sweet lips I am longing to taste,
Whose figure I imagine barely covered in silk and lace,
Woman who lives in my heart that is now her place?

When or Where to Write Poetry

One never knows when the urge to write a poem will manifest itself. **The next poem was penned when I was confined to my home, as a frightening storm raged outside.** Not only have I seen and heard, but I have also experienced the toppling effect that a broken heart has on a person's psyche and overall mental condition. Because of that I was able to symbolize the violence of the storm raging outside, to the tumultuous effect of an inner shattering conflict of a broken heart.

All this led to the writing of "Stormy Heart"

STORMY HEART

When smiles are regularly splashed across my face,
That means the interior of my heart is a warm and sunny place.
But the climate of my heart now has a dreary tone,
Following a "Dear John" message on my private telephone
Yes the love of my life just told me goodbye,
Now there is nothing else to do but to curl up and cry.
The tell tale anguish on my face mirrors in part,
The storm that now rages wildly within my heart.

Anguished frowns and desolate shadows that on my brow form,
Are really ominous dark clouds of my heart's growing storm.
Tears that streak my face with their salty stain,
Floods and numbs my heart, as therein, they fall as freezing rain.
The yellow, red, teary, glare of eyes filled with pain,
Register as twin bolts of lightning that set my heart aflame.
The sobs and groans that escape these lips time after time,
Are the sounds of thunder reverberating in this heart of mine.

When I tremble and stumble as if in drunken state,
It's just the shuddering caused by a catastrophic heartquake.
Tap water to wash the red from my eyes is what I crave
But it might engulf my heart as a destructive tidal wave.
I find a little relief in short patches of restless sleep,
There I'm in the eye of storm, but it's not for keeps.
Awaking in a dreadful sweat I realize that it's not a dream,
That the storm in my heart is still trucking along at full steam.

Strong I must be, for time I've been told will play a great part,
To help me weather the love sick gale winds that assault my heart.
So whatever comes, I may bend but I will not be broken,
For somewhere in time and space lies a harbor, a safe haven.
Then I will be free once again to cruise the highways of love,
With a heart that beats calm and gentle as the wings of a dove.
Dear God I pray, as this inner tumult departs,
Please keep me safe from another STORMY HEART.

Chapter 4:

Why write Poetry?

Poetry enhances the beauty of your world,
And also add richness to the lives of others.

<u>Why Write Poetry?</u>

We write poetry because it's a media thru which we can
Relate, translate and landscape
The full spectrum of the human condition,
Including,
Hopes and fears,
Laughter and tears,
Trials and tribulations,
Your faith, love and devotion,
Peace and war,
Chaos and order,
Heartbreak and sorrow,
Also your dreams of tomorrow,
Into beautiful words,
That can soothe, comfort, inspire and motivate
The human spirit.

<u>Why Write Poetry?</u>

A life lived is not one that is lived alone and separate. So many factors and so many people are involved in the making of a life.

It would be really incredible and mind numbing, if we ever tried to numerate all the factors and individuals that have influenced us, from the time of our birth to our golden sunset years.

<u>Why Write Poetry?</u>

It is such a poetic theme, that each life is different. That although some of our life experiences overlap, intersect and even interact, there will always be a unique factor to it.

We would need several lifetimes to write about the varied subjects that encompass our one chronological lifetime that ranges from the dawn of our lives to our sunset years.

Therein is the beauty and joy of writing poetry. We are never too young to write or too old to compose.

I would suggest that it is best to begin, by writing about our earliest memories, as they are so quick to fade. Topics may include a favorite toy, the first day at kinder garden school, a first playmate, or the first visit to Walt Disney World.

These would be the opening poems, in composing a poetic account on times of your life. Once again I repeat. One is never too young or too old to take this fascinating and rewarding journey into the art form that is poetry.

Why write Poetry?

We should write poetry because our lives were filled with lyrical content from the first moment of our birth.

Why Write Poetry?

We were all immersed in poetry from the very first day when we were born. Apart from nursing, it has proven to be the greatest source of comfort, throughout our earliest years.

Parents, grandparents and babysitters all over the world have used the recital of nursery rhymes to soothe and calm the minds of babies.

The most famous and time tested lullaby is

Quote…….*"Rockabye baby on the tree top*
      When the wind blows the cradle will rock"
End of quote.

As we got older and attended Pre-school, we were later introduced to some more of the popular rhymes like the following ones:

"Jack and Jill"

"Mary had a little lamb"

"Ole Macdonald had a farm"

Such poems live on, with a host of similarly entertaining ones that we still remember up to today, and now recite to our own little children.

Those clever lyrics helped shaped our young minds, and fostered our early imaginations.

Our assimilation into poetry continued throughout all levels of our education and adult life

Why write Poetry?

The world will never outgrow the need for additional rhymes for kids.

Why Write Poetry?

Many Iinternet companies are now offering personalized poems and other graphical forms of expressions, mainly directed at kids.

Since nobody remotely knows your kids better than you do, wouldn't it seem much more personal if you were to attempt to compose some lyrical lines about his or her behavioral inclinations that might indeed be unique to their budding personalities?

Their frolics and their behaviors as they continually discover the world around them, never cease to amaze and amuse us. Since you normally document those moments by taking pictures, so why not start taking it a step further by adding some thoughtful lines of verse.

Why write Poetry?

Write to celebrate the birth of new additions to the family.

Why Write Poetry?

The birth of my first grandchild affected me so profoundly, that I felt an undeniable urge to compose the following poem about her.

Kaleese

KALEESE, I have so many stories to tell you,
So much that I don't even know where to start.
But please know that already,
You occupy a very special place in my heart.

KALEESE, you are a bright promise for the future,
So innocent, Angelic and sweet,
Little Darling, I am your Grand Pop,
And you have made my life complete.

KALEESE, I am not known to you yet,
But when I finally do,
You will learn that there are no other girls I love,
More than your MOM and YOU

KALEESE, you are a gift to this family
From the heavens above,
And we will teach you all about GOD
And His boundless love.

Why write Poetry?

Many of us are often inspired by the incredible, captivating nature of our loved ones, and thus should take some time to pay tribute to them.

What Time Is It?

The sun was rising over the far yonder hills
As two little birds were singing on the window sills.
My wife also now awake adjusts my tie just a little bit,
While asking me what time is it.
I looked into her eyes so wide and blue,
And said darling it's always time to say I love you.

She said kneel with me it's time to pray,
And give thanks to God for a brand new day.
I will have your breakfast ready soon,
As she made her way to the children's room.
I hugged my wife and kids with a heavy sigh,
Kissing each soundly, as I bid them, my daily goodbye.

The break bell rang, about time, was the customary fret,
As my co-worker rushed outside to smoke a cigarette.
Grabbing my phone as it was my regular loving choice,
It was time hear the melody of my wife's sweet voice.
That and the sounds in the background of my kids at play,
Provide me with the will and energy to work each day.

The workday ends, my friends say let's stop for a beer,
But it was time to get home, I made that very clear.
They joked that my wife had all the home authority,
I cared not, being happy and in a haste to see my family.
They all greeted me at the door and the joy I felt,
Never once failed to cause this heart of mine to melt.

After making several solemn promises of not to peek,
My kids and I played many rounds of hide and seek.
It's time to wash for supper my wife soon said,
Then later time for a story as we tucked the kids in bed.
We thoroughly enjoyed a rerun of a classic comedy,
Further bonding while enjoying each others' company.

It was soon time for bed so we knelt to pray,
And thanked God for granting us another day.
I personally thanked Him for my wife's tender touch,
And for our kids whom we love so very much.
It was also time for us to reflect and meditate,
And pray for all those who were not as fortunate.

<u>*Why Write Poetry?*</u>

The teenage phase can be the most informative time of your life. It's a period in which we begin to define and mold ourselves into the persons that we are going to become.

It's at this stage of our life that there are many contradicting ideas being imputed into our minds, and thus, correct thought processing becomes an important issue.

By writing essays and poems about occurring incidents and ideas, would definitely promote proper decision making.

Why Write Poetry?

The everyday challenges that teenagers face, are varied and complex in nature. Therefore the topics for teenage poetry are too numerous to mention.

There are the adversities of high school and the resulting peer pressures. The drive to excel in academic and sporting events, along with negotiating the intimidating avenues of teenage romance, can provide very interesting subject matter for poetry.

Write about your parents, brothers and sisters and your no doubt evolving relationship with them, as you grow into adulthood.

The diary that you maintain is by all means for your personal perusal, but there maybe be some items in it that you would like to share and convert into a poetry format. For instance, subjects like your childhood friends, special events of holidays and celebrations.

Formatting your college and career choices into poetry would help to define your prospects, and may even provide fresh perspective into new avenues of options.

By constantly practicing your writing skills will keep your ideas organized in your mind, in your career and in your life.

Why write Poetry?

I find it therapeutic to write about the friends that I have made, and also about those that I have lost.
There is also a compelling urge to write about what I have learnt, concerning the virtues of friendship.

The upcoming poem is a about a young woman with whom I enjoyed a professional relationship, that then turned into a great friendship. She at that time worked for a company called JORO that was based in Miami.

Her name is Rossana, and so is the title of the poem, that is dedicated to her.

ROSSANA

R is for a ROSE, it's the first half of her name
The two main colors indicates her blossoming fame.
The white ROSE is her sweet nature
That is often beyond compare,
But beware the red ROSE,
It's her anger that many have come to fear.

O is for the OUTSTANDING woman that she is,
Completely devoted to her family and her kids.
Respected by her friends and co-workers it seems,
And even in New York we think that she is a dream

S is for SENORITA ESPANOL, from out of Brazil she came,
Speaking several languages as if they all were the same.
Her generosity to others I have seen time and time again,
But for me in the rear, she can often be a pain.

S is for the SUCCESS she seeks each and every day,
You can always count on her best effort, at work or play.
Joro is lucky to have her, I mean this with all my heart,
She makes difficult jobs look easy, this is an acquired art

A is for an ADVENTUROUS spirit, she shows it all the time,
Driving a Sports Mustang is beyond cool, it's so fine.
She races Ski Mobiles across the wide open seas?
She has more energy than a swarm of stinging bees.

N is for NICOTINE, oh yes she smokes more than a little bit,
But I'm hoping pretty soon, she decides it's time to quit.
I can't be too critical, as we all have habits that are wrong,
A little encouragement and soon she will quit before long.

A is for being an ANGEL who floated down from the sky,
With her as a friend we will all learn how to fly.
We are happy to have her here in the land of the free,
And for helping us to be the best that we can be.

Why write Poetry?

The world around us is constantly changing and evolving, and so should our thoughts and our ideas. It should be our duty and pleasure to write about our revolutionary thoughts. Here is one of mine that I call: Famous False Phrases

FAMOUS FALSE PHRASES

Many are the FALSE PHRASES we utter
Or hear from day to day,
But the insights that I now offer
May cause you to ponder the very next words you say.

The phrase FALLING IN LOVE
Is the most famous falsehood.
How can falling initiate an emotion
That keeps you feeling so high and good?

One flies, leaps or floats into love
Like a feather on a cushion of air.
While one FALLS only into heartbreak,
Which leads to sadness and despair

You see, falling denotes a low factor of negativity,
While Love abides in the high realm of positively.
So let us make the phrase FALLING IN LOVE
A notion of the past that is put to bed,
And let the words ELEVATING INTO LOVE,
Be universally adopted instead.

That "ALL IS FAIR IN LOVE AND WAR"
Is so far from the truth that it is a crime.
Love and war are opposing forces of our reality
Their engaging rules must stand the test of time.

Love stands for life but not at any cost.
War leads to death where innocent lives may be lost.
The pursuit of both must be honorable and just,
Or else victory in either will soon turn
Laughter into tears and tears into dust.

That "GOOD GUYS FINISH LAST"
Is such a pessimistic thought.
If we continue to accept this,
Then goodness would all be for naught.

Nice guys may not always get there first, my friend,
But sooner or later, they will win in the end.
Cream you see always rises to the top,
It's not always who catches the ball at the very first hop.

So guys hold your heads up high
And stand as tall as you can,
For being nice, gentle, genuine and sweet
Is what really makes you a man.

These are just a few of the falsies that I have put to the test.
There are many others, in time that I plan to address,
So please ponder what I've given you here and now,
As I continue working on all of the rest.

Why write Poetry?

The question about what love is and how it is defined has been with us for a very long time. However, regardless of the manner in which each and every one of us perceive it to be, we can all agree that it is the strongest force in the universe.

The format of poetry is the perfect platform to express our unique perceptions on what we think that love really is.

The following poem represents my personal observations.

Love Is A Very Big Word

There are many big words in the dictionary, but Oh wow!
None comes close to being as large as the one called LOVE.
It envelops a couple walking down a wedding aisle,
And it comes naturally between a parent and a child.
It's a lifetime bond between a brother and a sister,
And what unites a family into a self reliant cluster.

With only four letters, LOVE is still a very big word,
It can cut both ways like a two-edged sword.
For it can lift your wings and fly you to a better world,
Or it can torture your mind and devour your heart and soul.
It can cause you to be shy, or dares you to be bold,
Yet its full meaning and measure is yet to be told.

There is a universal language in the one word called love,
And none is more powerful here on earth or above.
It can be a wondrous sensation between a boy and his girl,
Or is a painful heartache when love starts to unfurl.
It can stimulate lovers to pursue shared dreams,
Or is a nightmare that rips your heart apart at the seams.

Love is all around us, it's between people and their pets,
It is even displayed on inanimate objects.
It's found in cars, houses and the fine clothes that we wear,
It's on jewels and the silverware that receive such great care.
It's focused on hobbies of each and every kind,
And it dictates the activities of our very valuable spare time.

Love is the answer to all our worldly problems and strife,
As its power can unite races, cultures and all religions of life
It can span barriers of age and just like fine wine,
Becoming richer and stronger thru the passage of time.
Love is a very big word, of this there is no doubt,
As no other word carries such a magnificent clout.

Why write Poetry?

We are always searching for ways in which to portray the extent and intensity of our love for someone.

Sometimes what is in our heart becomes very difficult to express in the spoken words, whereas, the underlying emotions seem to freely flow thru the written words.

Herein again is the joy of writing poetry.

Let My Love Be

Let my love be your anchor
In life's wild and stormy sea.
Let my love be naked and free,
Exposed for all the world to see.
You fill my life with such serenity,
Let my love be, let it, let it be.

I look forward to the future,
With us walking hand in hand,
Loving each other more and more,
Even as the hour glass shifts its sand.
May our light shine for all eternity,
Let my love be, let it, let it be.

I strive each day to better myself
In each and everything that I do,
And for all the successes that I've had,
There is no one else to thank but you.
Sometimes I stumble,
Though no need to call,
For you always seem to be there
To help me up whenever I fall.
You are always there for me,
Let my love be, let it, let it be.

Let us build a life of memories
That won't soon fade away,
So that when we are feeling a little too stiff
To do all the fun things that we did each day,
Then we can just sit back and relax,
As we rewind our minds for instant replay.
This is life's aging remedy
As time passes so swiftly,
Let my love be, let it, let it be.

Why write Poetry?

Here is another about the intricacies of love. It's my own fable on the pitfalls of not appreciating the gift of love that we sometimes hold in our hands, only to discover the virtues of it, once it is lost.

FREEDOM OF THE HEART

It would be a mistake to fall in love with me,
As I am only truly happy when single and free.
I am not a canary in a cage hanging in the air,
The songs I sing are for the whole world to hear.
I enjoyed providing the occasional flowers and wine,
But for me there can be no permanent ties of any kind.
Your lips are the sweetest I can honestly state,
Yet many are the others that I am longing to taste.
Our sweet encounter will forever be in my memory,
But I cannot seem to tame this constant urge to be free.

The far yonder hills are calling my name,
As there are many more adventures and frontiers to tame.
What destiny awaits me I just do not know,
There are so many paths that I feel inclined to follow.
Please think of me every once in a while,
And I hope when you do that your face springs a smile.
I am looking to the future and not what lies behind,
I'm thinking of women with just a good time on their minds.
Forever sweet and strong I hope that you will always be,
Completely understanding of my great need to be free.

FREEDOM OF THE HEART

Well, many dull and exciting places I have been,
And varied are the personalities I have met and seen.
But the years have just taught me a great lesson you see,
That single and care free is not what it's cracked up to be.
Your sweet nature just could not be eclipsed,
The memory now is as sweet as my first taste of your lips.
The compass of my heart has led me back to you,
And your heart is the only frontier I want to travel through.
How it hurts to discover that I've been back much too late,
I'm a prisoner of love, as you've since met your soul mate.

The moral of this story is very easy to define,
The freedom you are searching for lies buried in your mind.
The mysteries of a woman are so complex I've been told,
That you'd need more than a lifetime to see them unfurled.
So be sure to fully explore the gift in the hand that you hold,
The uniqueness that you'll reveal may open up a new world.
Simply said a sweetheart in the hand as such,
Is certainly worth more than two in the proverbial bush.
Searching for freedom the open road is not the place to start,
It's found thru the portals to your mind and your heart.
Not committing to the ties I found so very easy to decline,
Has made me a casualty of love who simply ran out of time.

Why write Poetry?

Countless are the poems that have been written about the heart. Apart from its physical duty of regulating the flow of blood throughout our body, it is the poetic home of all our emotional states.

It is the place where we feel love and heartache, happiness and sorrow.
It is also where dreams and hope reside.

The following is a poem of mine that hopefully shines some lights on this blessed phenomenon.

Cascading Hearts

I have a heart that loves and wants to be loved,
A heart that can sometimes fly to the stars above.
A heart that whispers, a heart that shouts,
A heart that is eager to learn what life is all about.

I have a heart that is sometimes lonely, sad and blue,
A heart that can be smart or simply without a clue.
A heart that is shy but sometimes dares to be bold,
A heart that cares for the helpless, the sick and the old.

I have a heart that cries when the movies are sad,
A heart that leaps for joy whenever good conquers bad.
A heart that jumps and sometimes skip a beat,
A heart that dreams of a love that is rich and sweet.

I have a heart that races and sometimes beat too fast,
A heart that is searching for a love that will last.
A heart whose search is over, for a love that is true,
A heart that is in heaven since the day that I met you.

I have a heart that now dances with yours in sheer delight,
A rhythmic motion of hearts ever ready to take flight.
It's a heart that cascades into an infinite number of hearts,
Each with its own heartfelt emotional message to impart.

Why write Poetry?

We are often deluged by all the news that is happening around the world, and I think that we are obligated to record our personal views of the humane and geo-political state of the world, in a poetical format.

THE UNBORN BABY WONDERS

Safe and warm in her mother's womb,
An unborn baby's mind develops and starts to bloom.
Immediately her love to her host she surrenders.
But heeding her evolutionary instincts,
She ponders and she wonders
Did my mother abstain from alcohol, cigarettes and drugs?
So when I'm born my operating systems will be free of bugs?
Will my father be there to guide, protect and support,
Or will be a deadbeat dad being frowned on by the courts?

As the unborn baby anticipates her impending birth,
She wonders on the state of mother earth.
Are they still polluting every single breath of fresh air?
And depleting the ozone that protects the atmosphere?
Are the rainforest still being cleared for industry and wealth
Without any regards for the next generation's health?
Have they started protecting the animals that live in the wild
Or still wantonly hunting them for sport and for style?
Will the whales be still singing their mournful songs?
Or driven to the edge of extinction before long?

THE UNBORN BABY WONDERS

Conserving her energy the little baby slumbers,
But even in her dreams the unborn baby wonders.
Is the African Nation still divided by boundaries and wars?
Or can they finally brag,
That they are now one land, one government,
One people and one flag?
The Middle East, the land that Jesus walked,
Is it still the world's center of senseless violence and hate?
Or have the Jews, Arabs and Muslims living peacefully,
And being respectful each other's faith?
Did Dr. Martin Luther King's Dream finally come to pass?
Are FREEDOM and EQUALITY being enjoyed by all at last?

The unborn baby awakes kicking her mother's stomach with glee,
As she anticipates God's many wondrous creations to see,
The blue skies, the flowers, the birds and colors of the rainbow,
Days that fade into night, the twinkling stars, and the moon glow.
But soon, a tiny frown etches upon her little face,
As she wonders about the many horrors, still taking place.
Is violence still on the increase among the youths of today?
Are they not listening to the words that crime does not pay?
Are they still being exposed to drugs and guns at a tender age?
Are kids killing kids the highlight on each newspaper front page?

As the unborn baby anticipates her impending birth,
She wonders and ponders on the state of mother earth.

THE UNBORN BABY WONDERS

THE UNBORN BABY WONDERS
(PART TWO)

As the unborn baby flexes her tiny limbs in the womb,
She is comforted by the gentle sound of her mother's heart,
The pulsing, that echoes off the walls of her warm cocoon.
But suddenly the unborn baby twitches,
Visions of terror forecast a frightening apocalyptic gloom.
Atomic weapons developed by unstable governments,
Now in the clutches of terrorists, spell a sure nuclear doom.

Her happy dream state is abruptly ripped asunder,
Causing her once again to worry and wonder.
Are suicide bombers, exploding school busses and airplanes
Now the normal agenda for some nightmarish master plan?
She is praying that it's just be a bad dream,
Not the sad reality of man's escalating inhumanity to man.
Soon to be delivered into this hostile, unsafe outside world,
The unborn baby shivers with a bitter and chilly cold.

As the unborn baby anticipates her impending birth,
She wonders and ponders on the state of mother earth.

Why write Poetry?

None among us have reached the age of maturity without having our hearts broken at some time or the other.
Even though in retrospect, that such affair was not one that was good for us, we however, cannot deny that even though it was a lesson that was learned, it still was truly a very traumatic time of our lives.

This was a benchmark period.
It's a part of what made us who we are.
So why not write about it?

When the wind blows through

There is a hole in my heart
That was left by you.
And it hurts like hell
When the wind blows through.

When the wind blows through

The winds of a hurricane are dangerous,
If caught in one you'll know what I mean.
However, sooner or later,
They will normally run out of steam
But here in my heart there is no end in sight
From these everlasting winds of pain,
That cause my tears to sting my cheeks,
Like torrential windblown rain.
Yes, there is a hole in my heart,
From a love that was untrue.
And it hurts like hell,
When the painful wind blows through.

The winds of war
That blow from time to time,
Can often be calmed
By the prevailing peaceful minds.
But these unending winds of sorrow
Blow like there'll never be another tomorrow.
There is this hole in my heart
A heart that was true to you.
And it hurts like hell,
When that sad wind blows through.

The winds of loneliness
Chill me to the bone.
I am lost and confused,
And never felt so much alone.
You ripped a hole in my heart,
The heart that was faithful to you,
Now it hurts like hell,
When the lonely wind blows through.

Why write Poetry?

America is involved in wars on several fronts, all because we lead the world in the seemingly, never ending struggle for basic international human rights. We all think alike I'm quite sure, that if another citizen of this world suffers in a degradingly human manner, that it somewhat diminishes our own human awareness and rights.

Many of our men and women, willing risk their lives each and every day, fighting to correct this ignoble problem.

I regard it as a privilege to honor them and their families thru my poetry.

The Brave Young soldier

On a hot and dusty desert dawn
A brave young soldier dies.
And on a cold and dreary Montana morn
A grieving mother cries.

He was planning on starting college in the fall,
But when terror struck he answered the call.
On the dangers of war he was fully aware,
But in defense of freedom his duty was very clear.

The grenade arced in out of the clear blue sky.
And there was nothing else to do but to pray and die.
He leapt smothering the bomb with his torso,
Completely absorbing the shrapnel flow.

His brave sacrifice was successfully applied,
As all the nearby soldiers miraculously survived.
With solemn salutes they bid their hero goodbye,
As tears of grief and admiration filled each swollen eye.

By dawn's early light
Many brave soldiers fight for human dignity.
While on a midsummer night
Families hope and pray for their abiding safety.

Why write Poetry?

Every day we see and hear of people, young and old, who are lost in their own personal misery. Most are products of their own making, and others because of bad luck and an uncaring society. When it's possible, let us reach out and help someone, even if it is the form of poetry.

The joy or writing poetry forever lies in the touching of someone's life for the good.

The Good Girl Gone Bad

You were once a good girl
Nice and sweet in every way,
But constant abuse has led you
Further and further astray,
You have been often fooled,
Used and abandoned with a sorry goodbye.
You're now a good girl gone bad,
Who is now living only for the next false high.

The Good Girl Gone Bad

Memories of the girl you once were,
Is completely lost in a drug induced blur.
Your new reality which is now buried
In the darkness of your mind,
Has left you forsaken
Without hope or help of any kind.

But deep within you blank gaze,
I sense a real wanting to escape
From your drowsy haze.
I glimpse a lonely solitary spark of desire
A desperate needing of someone,
To help you ignite that self restoring fire.

I will do all that I can to assist you,
In the restoring of your lost world.
It won't be easy overcoming the drugs
Or being forgiven for all that that you stole.
Also the road back will be difficult
And so full of pain,
But persevere as there is so much
Of your good life to be regained.

I saw the beauty behind that gaunt face,
I saw the inner struggle
Of a lost path to retrace,
I saw a girl, to whom life was unfair,
And I saw the girl
I forever want my whole life to share.

Why write Poetry?

Imagination is often said to be good for the soul. The "Getting Iffy with It" poem below, is my semi-serious uptake on the subject

Getting " Iffy" with it

Caught up in a fantasy world
About you and I not too long ago
When Will Smith's "Get Jiggy wid it"
Started playing on the radio.
Since I was imagining,
IF I was this and IF you were that,
The phrase, "GETTIN IFFY WITH IT"
Crossed my mind in no time flat.

So, if I was jack
And you were Jill,
We would climb to the top
Of Blueberry Hill,
And there under the moon
And stars shining bright,
We would savor our thrill
All thru the long night.

Getting " Iffy" with it

IF you were that little girl,
Red Riding Hood,
I would battle the Bad Wolf
Who was up to no good.
Seeing myself as your Knight
In white shining armor,
Comfortable in the role
Of being your lifelong protector.

IF you were a star sailing
Across the dark and lonely sky,
I would be a carpet of stardust
Upon which you can safely fly.
We would travel to far away galaxies,
Yet unseen by human eyes,
Lighting a path of perfect romance,
For when others in love pass by.

IF you were a pretty little bird
Caught up in a hurricane
I would be an eagle whose wings would
Protect you from the wind and the rain.
I would circle forever
In the calm eye of the storm,
So that you would be safe with me
Until the gale winds were gone.

Getting " Iffy" with it

IF you were a butterfly fluttering
Around in the vicinity of my heart,
Each heart beat would vibrate your wings
With an emotional message to impart.
Their rhythmic symphony
Would be a musical expression,
A continuous, cascading echo
Of my eternal love and devotion.

If it's God's wish that
I go to Heaven before you do,
To watch over you I would request
A room with an earth bound view
So that when the final
Trumpet call comes due,
I would be at the Lord's side,
Helping Him hold out His hand to you.

So even though Will Smith says
"JIGGY" is the way to go,
I find that "GETTIN IFFY"
Will soon be quite as popular.
For imagination is said to be
Good for your virtual soul,
As it maximizes your equilibrium,
Here in the real world.

Why write Poetry?

When we shop for well wishing cards, we spend an inordinate amount time opening up numerous cards, in order to find the one that most closely portray our own sentiment.

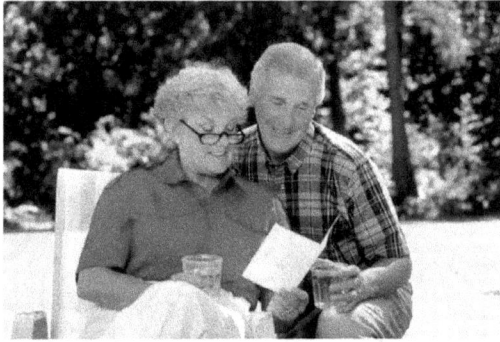

Why write Poetry?

Creating your own well wishing cards.

The joy of writing poetry allows us to accurately express our personal feelings. Our current level of technology provides many free or inexpensive programs that currently provide access to thousands of art and pictures that can be edited into your homemade cards

There is no age limit to this creative activity that can prove to be a fun one for the entire family.

Please note that anyone with an applicable computer program can create an original card, but the overriding love and desire to write poetry, is the major force that drives this activity.

This project can even be expanded to include friends, maybe even form a Card Creating Club. The final productions can ultimately be offered up for sale to card making companies.

Why write Poetry?

In the same manner that we seek out just the right card, we often find ourselves looking for the exact graphic tee shirt that expresses our own unique personalities, or those of our family members and friends.

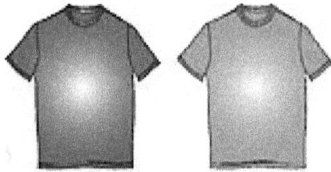

Why write Poetry?

<u>Designing Your Own Graphic Tee Shirts.</u>

Most of the poetry that we compose is built around one or several catchy phrases. Some of these may be phrases that we might like to see emblazoned on our personal tee shirts.

Once again your composed lines of poetry, along with free internet graphic images, or the use of personal drawings, and or photographs, can certainly set the stage for designing your own individualized tee shirts.

Just like the Card Creation in the previous chapter, this can also grow into a family or group activity, which may also evolve into a business enterprise.

The simple method for this, involves printing your image on widely available contact paper, making sure that the reverse image is printed instead the face up one. This printout is then laid face down on the front of your tee shirt, then applying an ironing machine on the back of the paper to transfer the images. Using another printout, an image can also be applied to the back of a shirt. This operation is known as HEAT TRANSFER.

There are also affordable heat transfer appliances available that can simplify and speed up this operation.

Why write Poetry?

Imagine using extracts from your own poetry compositions to create your own unique graphic tee shirts. You can even write lines that are specific for tee shirt printing.

The blending of poetical phrases and slangs are limitless. Your lyrical compositions can be humorous, serious or politically oriented, and can be printed on a many types of garments or fabrics. Baby and adult aprons, pillowcases, tabletop covers, placement mats, handkerchiefs and thermal wear can all be printed with words from your mini poetry compositions.

Why write Poetry?

One of the main reasons for writing poetry is the pleasure of sharing the compositions with others. We normally commence doing so, by passing copies around.

Let your poems be read all around the world.

Why write Poetry?

Post Your Poems.

You have spent a great deal of time, effort and love creating your poems, and just as an artist's joy collimates in seeing his efforts displayed, so too, should you rejoice in the sharing of your poetical efforts. Unlike a personal diary, your lyrical lines should be for the whole world to share.

In this ultra modern world, there are many ways to achieve this. The first is to post your poems on Face Book, Twitter or any of the other social networks that you are connected to. The resulting feedback will be invaluable to your future projects,

There are also dedicated internet sites that allow you to freely upload your poems, so that the general public can log in and search for your poems, either by the titles or the name of the Author. This is truly important, as, the network recognizes and protects your copy write and your ownership of the poems. You can access this user friendly website at:

www.poetry.com

This website is continually running poetical contests, which are open to the general public. It is a very simple procedure to upload and submit your poems.

Why write Poetry?

Getting published

One of the greatest pleasures that I have experienced, was the time that I saw the first publication of one of my poems in print.

That particular poem appeared in several local newspapers, and the feedback that I received from family, friends and acquaintances, left me with an incredible joyous feeling.

Why write Poetry?

<u>Becoming A Published Poet.</u>

After my first newspaper publishing I felt motivated to expand my publishing endeavors. I started by selecting about ten to fifteen of my favorite compositions, created a stylized cover, made fifty copies and with the aid of a stapling machine, I found myself with fifty copies of my home self-published poetry booklet.

Those early activities led to my mainstream publications. It would be prudent of you, the budding poet, to navigate the social networks, and search for others with similar poetical inclinations, and form some type of publication club. Thus, the publishing costs would be minimized, by sharing the expenses with others.

There are many affordable self publishing companies around, which can be found through GOOGLE or any other online search machines..

Why write Poetry?

Writing poetry can lead to Writing a novel

Why write Poetry?

Becoming A Novelist.

The confidence gained in composing and publishing your poetry may cause you to ponder the possibility of expanding your writing ability, towards developing a novel.

It is widely known that many established authors begun their writing careers by composing poetry, and many will confess that they still do. Becoming a novelist does not mean that you have lost the joy of writing poetry, as the two formats complement each other.

Some of your poetry titles may indeed lend themselves to novelizations

Why write Poetry?

Writing poetry can lead to Writing a hit song

Why write Poetry?

<u>Becoming A Song Writer.</u>

With a little tweaking here and there, one of your written poems may indeed be the lyrics of a song that others would love listening to. If knowledge of music is one of your talents, then your poetry book may even be your songbook.

If you think that some of your poems would sound good as potential songs, but you do not know how to write music, then try asking a friend or an acquaintance to do so for you.

There are also websites that offer payments for posted lyrics that can be transformed into musical renditions.

These are just a few of the themes that your joy of writing poetry can evolve into.

Why write Poetry?

We can use our poetry in the
composing of motivational phrases
for the uplifting of human and
community spirits and morality.

Why write Poetry?

<u>Make A Social Impact With Wise Phrases.</u>

Create meaningful one, two or three liners with compelling words of advice. Many times we have been moved by the motivational elements in the words on bumper stickers and posters.

Let your written lines be an energizing force of good on the many negative prevailing issues that plague your community.

The problems that need highlighting are many and varied. Here are some of the fundamental issues:

Driving under the influence of alcohol or drugs.

Driving and Texting.

Drug addiction.

Child abuse.

Deadbeat dads.

Teenage pregnancies.

The High School dropout rate.

Bullying.

Guns on the streets

Discriminations of all kinds.

Going green.

These are just a sample of topics that be focused upon.

Why write Poetry?

<u>Make A Social Impact With Wise Phrases.</u>

Please note that you don't have to go it alone. You can start by creating or borrowing some lines from your previously written poems, then you can enlist the help of some of your friends to brainstorm and expand on your ideas. With the aid of some added graphics, your created phrases on banners and stickers can be displayed in prominent places, to be a motivational cause for the betterment of society.

To get you started, below are a couple of them that I wrote.

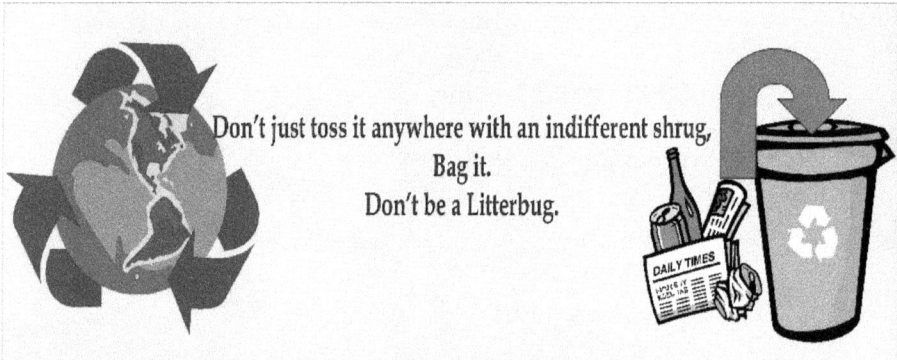

Don't just toss it anywhere with an indifferent shrug,
Bag it.
Don't be a Litterbug.

****

When he or she TEXT and DRIVES,
They are playing
Russian roulette with innocent LIVES

****

Why write Poetry?

Writing poetry is a fun activity for everyone, from ages nine to ninety nine and beyond.

Why write Poetry?

Because It's A Fun Activity For All Ages.

There is definitely no age limits for discovering the joy of writing poetry. Kinder garden kids enjoy seeing their written notes about mom, dad and the baby stuck upon the door of the fridge.

Many teenage romances have begun with the scribbling of heartfelt words on their notepads. These are the early joyful moments of writing poetry.

For the mature and the elderly, it is a peaceful activity that can be indulged in, either at home or during the time spent at a park. Writing poetry is a wonderful way to relive some old memories, to refocus on past events in the changing times of their lives.

The joy of writing poetry is a never ending experience.

The end

Sources of poetical enlightenment.

Creating Poetry..............by John Drury

Poetry in the Making....by Ted Hughes

Graded Ebonii...........by Ebonii

About the Author.

I am part of a close knit family, with three sisters, five brothers, a daughter, two grandchildren, and a large number of extended relatives.

I'm from the beautiful, Caribbean Island of St.Kitts, is single and currently resides in Brooklyn, New York.

I've successfully finished three full New York City marathons and over twenty half marathons, but I have not entered either for several years. However, I am now training hard to be ready for this year's 2014, running of the NYC marathon.

 Meanwhile I am also working on:

PoemScapes: A Pictorial Illustration of Poetry,

A children's book, and

A not yet titled Action Novella.

All of which are due out in 2014.

I can be contacted at **(poemscapes@aol.com)**

My family will probably be a little embarrassed that I inserted the following family photo, but I just could not help myself………**I am totally inspired by them.**

www.ingramcontent.com/pod-product-compliance
Lightning Source LLC
Chambersburg PA
CBHW071001040426
42443CB00007B/615